HOLIDAY HISTORY
JUNETEENTH

by J.P. Miller

pogo

Ideas for Parents and Teachers

Pogo Books let children practice reading informational text while introducing them to nonfiction features such as headings, labels, sidebars, maps, and diagrams, as well as a table of contents, glossary, and index.

Carefully leveled text with a strong photo match offers early fluent readers the support they need to succeed.

Before Reading

- "Walk" through the book and point out the various nonfiction features. Ask the student what purpose each feature serves.
- Look at the glossary together. Read and discuss the words.

Read the Book

- Have the child read the book independently.
- Invite him or her to list questions that arise from reading.

After Reading

- Discuss the child's questions. Talk about how he or she might find answers to those questions.
- Prompt the child to think more. Ask: Juneteenth is a celebration of freedom. Can you name any other celebrations of freedom?

Pogo Books are published by Jump!
5357 Penn Avenue South
Minneapolis, MN 55419
www.jumplibrary.com

Copyright © 2024 Jump! International copyright reserved in all countries. No part of this book may be reproduced in any form without written permission from the publisher.

Library of Congress Cataloging-in-Publication Data

Names: Miller, J. P. (Janice P.), author.
Title: Juneteenth / J. P. Miller.
Description: Minneapolis, MN: Jump!, Inc., 2024.
Series: Holiday history | Includes index.
Audience: Ages 7-10
Identifiers: LCCN 2022059579 (print)
LCCN 2022059580 (ebook)
ISBN 9798885244572 (hardcover)
ISBN 9798885244589 (paperback)
ISBN 9798885244596 (ebook)
Subjects: LCSH: Juneteenth–Juvenile literature. Slaves–Emancipation–Texas–Juvenile literature. African Americans–Anniversaries, etc.–Juvenile literature. | African Americans–Social life and customs–Juvenile literature. | Slaves–Emancipation–United States–Juvenile literature.
Classification: LCC E185.93.T4 M555 2024 (print)
LCC E185.93.T4 (ebook)
DDC 394.263–dc23/eng/20221214
LC record available at https://lccn.loc.gov/2022059579
LC ebook record available at https://lccn.loc.gov/2022059580

Editor: Eliza Leahy
Designer: Molly Ballanger

Photo Credits: Shutterstock, cover; Twinsterphoto/Shutterstock, 1; DyrElena/Shutterstock, 3; Keith Lance/iStock, 4; THEPALMER/Getty, 5; incamerastock/Alamy, 6-7; Photo 12/Universal Images Group/Getty, 8-9; Sarah Reingewirtz/MediaNews Group/Los Angeles Daily News/Getty, 10; Khadejeh Nikouyeh/News & Record/AP Images, 11; Go Nakamura/Getty, 12-13; Brandon Bell/Getty, 14-15; Michael M. Santiago/Getty, 16-17; Paul Moseley/Fort Worth Star-Telegram/Tribune News Service/Getty, 18; Amanda McCoy/Fort Worth Star-Telegram/Tribune News Service/Getty, 19; Leonard Ortiz/MediaNews Group/Orange County Register/Getty, 20-21; aquariagirl1970/Shutterstock, 23 (left); gowithstock/Shutterstock, 23 (right).

Printed in the United States of America at Corporate Graphics in North Mankato, Minnesota.

TABLE OF CONTENTS

CHAPTER 1
Emancipation Day..4

CHAPTER 2
Juneteenth Traditions..10

CHAPTER 3
Juneteenth in the United States..................18

QUICK FACTS & TOOLS
Juneteenth Place of Origin............................22
Quick Facts...22
Glossary...23
Index..24
To Learn More...24

CHAPTER 1

EMANCIPATION DAY

Cannons shook the ground. Smoke filled the air. The year was 1862. The United States was in the middle of the **Civil War** (1861–1865). Troops from the North fought to end **slavery**. Troops from the South fought to keep it.

Slavery started more than 200 years before the war. White men **enslaved** Africans and brought them to America. People paid money for them. They forced them to work hard for no pay and treated them **cruelly**. Enslaved people wanted freedom.

CHAPTER 1

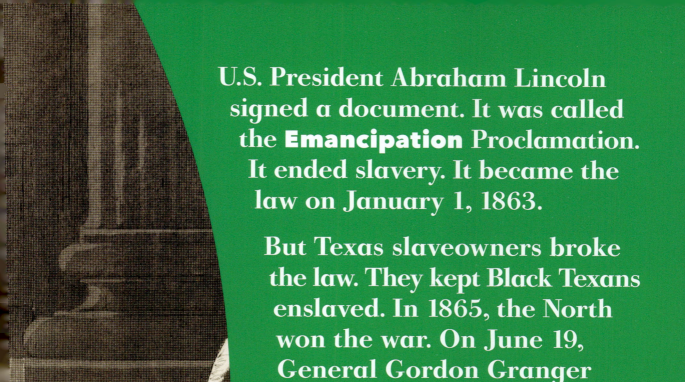

U.S. President Abraham Lincoln signed a document. It was called the **Emancipation** Proclamation. It ended slavery. It became the law on January 1, 1863.

But Texas slaveowners broke the law. They kept Black Texans enslaved. In 1865, the North won the war. On June 19, General Gordon Granger gave an order. Texans had to free all enslaved people.

Emancipation Proclamation

Newly freed Black people celebrated. They called it Emancipation Day. It was a celebration of freedom. People laughed and cried. They sang and danced. They played harmonicas. They cooked on open fires. They set tables with their favorite foods. This was the start of a **tradition**. The day is now known as Juneteenth.

DID YOU KNOW?

The name Juneteenth combines the month and date enslaved Texans were told of their freedom.

CHAPTER 1

CHAPTER 2

JUNETEENTH TRADITIONS

The event spread across the country. It is celebrated every year on June 19. Some events last several days! Sports teams play. Drummers beat African drums. DJs play music. People dance.

Family and friends gather. They enjoy barbecues. Fireworks light up the sky.

CHAPTER 2

People watch parades. Marching bands play. Everything is decorated in red, black, green, and gold.

CHAPTER 2

TAKE A LOOK!

The colors of Juneteenth **symbolize** Africa. Take a look!

■ = the people of Africa
■ = their **bloodshed**
■ = the riches of Africa
■ = the land

CHAPTER 2   13

Many people attend church. They celebrate the unbreakable **faith** of enslaved people. **Gospel** choirs sway, clap, and sing.

CHAPTER 2

Juneteenth is a time to remember the past. It is also a time to think about the future. People speak about **racial injustice**, jobs, and **health care**. They discuss important issues for Black people in the United States.

WHAT DO YOU THINK?

Some people walk or run 2.5 miles (4.0 kilometers) on Juneteenth. It is in honor of the 2.5 years enslaved Texans did not know slavery was over. What is another way we could honor those who were enslaved?

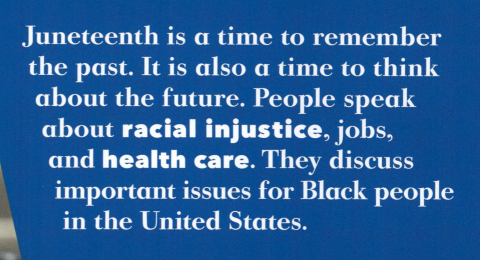

CHAPTER 2

CHAPTER 3
JUNETEENTH IN THE UNITED STATES

Juneteenth is the oldest African American celebration. Opal Lee grew up in Texas. She went to Juneteenth celebrations with her family all her life. She led the call for it to become a **national holiday**.

Opal Lee

Lee started a **petition**. More than 1 million people signed it. In 2016, 90-year-old Lee walked from Texas to Washington, D.C. She made stops along the way. She talked on radio and television shows.

CHAPTER 3   19

On June 17, 2021, it finally happened. President Joseph Biden and Vice President Kamala Harris made Juneteenth a national holiday.

Many businesses close for the holiday. People celebrate. Freedom is a win for everyone!

WHAT DO YOU THINK?

People of other **races** helped free enslaved African Americans. Do you think people of other races should celebrate Juneteenth? Why or why not?

CHAPTER 3　21

QUICK FACTS & TOOLS

JUNETEENTH PLACE OF ORIGIN

QUICK FACTS

Date: June 19

Year of Origin: 1865

Place of Origin: Galveston, Texas

Common Symbols: Juneteenth flag, American flag, red, black, green, and gold colors, red, white, and blue colors

Foods: hamburgers, hot dogs, chips, potato salad, baked beans, cakes, pies, soda, lemonade, sweet tea

Traditions: parades, fireworks, speeches, sports contests, concerts, barbecues

GLOSSARY

bloodshed: The injury or killing of humans, particularly as a result of war.

Civil War: The war between the Confederacy and the Union that took place in the United States between 1861 and 1865. The two sides fought over slavery, states' rights, and economic policies, among other issues.

cruelly: Done in a way that causes injury, grief, or pain.

emancipation: The act of freeing a person or group from slavery or control.

enslaved: Describing a person taken against their will and forced to work without pay.

faith: Belief in a god, system, or religion.

gospel: A style of African American religious singing.

health care: The system of medical care provided to individuals or a community.

national holiday: A legal holiday established by the federal laws of a nation.

petition: A written request for change signed by many people.

races: Groups into which human beings can be divided based on similar physical characteristics, such as skin color.

racial injustice: When a person is treated unfairly based on their race.

slavery: A system in which people enslave others.

symbolize: To stand for or represent something else.

tradition: A custom, idea, or belief that is handed down from one generation to the next.

QUICK FACTS & TOOLS

INDEX

Africa 13
barbecues 11
Biden, Joseph 20
church 14
Civil War 4, 5, 7
colors 12, 13
danced 8, 10
Emancipation Day 8
Emancipation Proclamation 7
fireworks 11
freedom 5, 7, 8, 20
Granger, Gordon 7
Harris, Kamala 20
Lee, Opal 18, 19
Lincoln, Abraham 7
music 10
national holiday 18, 20
parades 12
races 20
racial injustice 17
sang 8, 14
slavery 4, 5, 7, 17
Texas 7, 18, 19
tradition 8
United States 4, 17
Washington, D.C. 19

TO LEARN MORE

Finding more information is as easy as 1, 2, 3.
1. Go to www.factsurfer.com
2. Enter "Juneteenth" into the search box.
3. Choose your book to see a list of websites.

QUICK FACTS & TOOLS

INDEX

aquariums, 20
barbels, 10, 11
bodies, 8
colors, 8
critically endangered, 18
dams, 18, 19
eggs, 15
eyes, 9
food, 10, 12, 13
habitat, 4, 12, 18
identify, 11
Mekong River, 4, 5, 12, 14, 16, 20
migrate, 15
mouths, 10
name, 4

overfishing, 18, 19
people, 19, 20
pollution, 18
range, 4, 5, 14
record catch, 17
size, 6, 7, 9, 10, 16, 17
skin, 8
Southeast Asia, 5
spawn, 15, 18
stats, 21
teeth, 10
young, 10, 12, 16, 17

The images in this book are reproduced through the courtesy of: Lisa Angeline123, cover (hero); Rocksweeper, pp. 2-3, 22-23, 24 (background); Danny Ye, pp. 4-5, 11; Mike Towers, p. 4 (Mekong River); Stbernardstudio, pp. 6-7; Bill Roque, pp. 8, 8-9, 11 (gray and white body, big mouth), 12; tristan tan, pp. 10, 13, 16-17; slpu9945, p. 11 (small eyes); wk1003mike, pp. 14-15; Raymond Shiu, p. 15; Michael Greenfelder/ Alamy, pp. 18-19; ONUTTO, p. 20; Tambe/ Wiki Commons, pp. 20-21; ASSOCIATED PRESS/ AP Newsroom, p. 21.

TO LEARN MORE

AT THE LIBRARY

Davies, Monika. *Vietnam*. Minneapolis, Minn.: Bellwether Media, 2023.

Dufresne, Emilie. *Endangered Animals in the Rivers*. New York, N.Y.: Rosen Publishing, 2022.

Mattern, Joanne. *Giant Barbs*. Minneapolis, Minn.: Bellwether Media, 2024.

ON THE WEB

FACTSURFER

Factsurfer.com gives you a safe, fun way to find more information.

1. Go to www.factsurfer.com.

2. Enter "Mekong giant catfish" into the search box and click 🔍.

3. Select your book cover to see a list of related content.